This is my heart fully open for you, the
sorrow, the tears, the darkness and
sadness but also the joy, the laughter,
the feeling of fulfillment and the bright
sparks of our world
A small part of this world but every part
of me

AF208550

Loneliness
The devil and the salvor

A piece of my heart is within all of these
pages

Gabriel Hasbo

Förlag: BoD – Books on Demand, Stockholm, Sverige
Tryck: BoD – Books on Demand, Norderstedt, Tyskland
ISBN: 978-91-7569-157-2

Contents

Chapter One
Already Gone
The Sorrow

Seeing myself in the eyes is my worst
fear, nothing terrifies me as much as my
dark eyes digging into my own soul

Our lives will contain death more than once, there will be no hope for us though death is all we know and all that ever existed, death is the only thing in our lives that we can trust though it will always come to you even if you are not ready

No love last forever there is always an
expiration date for love, love can die
with us even though it often dies long
before we do

I`ve been broken, i`ve been hurt and my
life has been demolished right in front of
my eyes time and time again for love,
Nothing hurts as much as love can do
and that's the thing with love it almost
kills you

The love that I have can never be returned because the love of others never seems to be within my reach for me to feel it

I want to scream until my voice gets
tired of hearing itself, I want to cry until
my heart is flooded, I want to bleed out
all my frustration til there is no blood
left. My heart is about to explode, all the
emotions running through my body
makes me feel trapped within myself

- My inner pain

Why am I still here, why can't anyone see me anymore. I'm too afraid to look inside of me of what lies buried beneath the ground in the dark and is still alive

My head is a mess, my life is chaos, no
one can see me while i'm about to fall
down and spend the rest of my time
where the world's end lies

A fight has begun and the end of it is
long gone
if you are quick enough you might catch
it for else a full on war will rise and
death will be upon us all

You see my eyes
you see my shadows
you see my broken scars
you see how fragile I am and yet you
run from me

- My own mind

You see my eyes as they stare at you
you hear my voice growling in your ear
you can feel my presence being bored
but for you it's like I never was born

Say my name a hundred times and you
will never see me again, say it once and
I will be there

The tunnel to my heart is easy to find
but the deeper you go less you will find
and soon you will be lost in there
forever

The dark days are upon us soon
For me the days of darkness have
never left

There are three faces of me
The one I show you
The one I show my closest ones and
the one I never even show myself

No one in this world is coming for you
You better stand up quickly or be ready
to be picked down

No one has ever truly known me, I have never poured my heart out to anyone. This piece is my heart, soul and everything I have ever been. There is no one that knows who my soul is, who I really am. No one knows what demons lays beneath the layers of destruction. What has caused all of the pain that no one has ever seen. Things people see in their nightmares is what I see when I'm awake. There is a monster that lives and breathes within me all of the time and will do so until I surrender

Home

I am gone, I am gone from the place I once called home. I will never see you again cause I am going to the land I am from to the land I was born to the land I will die in. We will never meet again in the land I once called home in the land I once had hopes in, from the land I once had my dreams. My soul is missing. I have to leave this place cause I am already dead here

The days are getting shorter but the
nights feel like an eternity

The grip you hold around my heart is
what gets me out of bed
I`ll thank you for it but one day it will be
over

You say you want me, you say you love me but no actions you do speaks to me as your words do. You tell me you'd do anything for me and yet you have never done anything to prove it. Hold in the tears you shed for me for you are not worthy of feeling sorry about what you have done. Save your words and your regrets for someone that will never love you the way I have, you will not feel it today or tomorrow but one day you will realize the things i`d do for you

Nothing is at its place, everything has disappeared from its place and so have I. My eyes are open but they can not see, my mouth speaks but no sound can be heard, I`m lost within myself therefore I can't express who I am

I don't want to die but I want to give up, all I do is for nothing and none of the things I do takes me forward. The worst is that I have nothing to lose. Thinking about death and giving up always made me stand up and work harder but now all I want is to lay down and not wake up

Send me down to the chambers of hell
and leave me there
Let me die
Let me be buried down there
Let me grow back up so I can see the
stars one last time

I don't know how to live but I do know how to die. The days are coming and going but forward I ain't moving, I stand and stomp but my legs can't seem to take me forward, could this be the end of all the suffering for anything living I have never experienced. I hear heavy breaths in my ears, I see phantoms in the shadows and I feel the cold wherever I go. It is a man who stands and waits to take me to his dungeon, dead I will be shortly but the time I still have left I have no use for. Anything that has ever followed me in life is death, life has only slipped out of my hands my entire life without even experiencing any of it

I shield my wounds from the pain,
I have these scars that can't seem to
heal,
I open my eyes hoping the next day will
be better

No words are enough to heal a broken
heart
To solve a mistake or fix a trust that has
been broken
No words are enough

The words of my own voice kills me
time and time again
They drown me
They silence me
They choke me till my words disappear
forever

Emptiness is within all of my bones
It's rooted in my heart and pumped out
through my veins
It's all I feel and all I know

Day after day my life disappears more
and more
Dragged in the dirt into the next day I
move
Fighting for my life has left my body
ages ago and nothing here can keep
me alive anymore

Deep down the hole we go, the barrel is slowly moving from side to side, water dripping on the mountain walls and the drop down is bottomless, Nowhere to go but down, nowhere to move but to stay in the cold barrel, nowhere to see for the small light we have the dark eats up, darkness and death around us day in and day out, why do we do this to ourselves for the world for us never gets any better, the world for us can only be seen as a dark deep and wet hole

The days leave me one by one and
soon I will be left here all alone
I fear the day when I will wake up but I
will not see the sunset ever again

I see no world for us anymore
Time has passed and our tears have
dried up a long time ago
We wanted a place that we created
A place where we could have been free
and instead all of our life ended up with
our hearts broken

I live and breath with my death
Side by side it is with me everywhere I
go
No room to escape
No time to leave it behind
No world exist where it does not follow
me

My tears want to pour out of me
I fight to keep them in for they hurt so
much when they are dripping down my
cheeks
The pain within me is unbearable
I`m waiting to be reborn but the reborn
me is all pain that I can`t escape

I don`t think i`ll ever find a place where I
won't be lonely
Correction
I know I will always feel lonely
I`m a lost soul who can`t find his way
back home and i`ll stay like that till I die

I`ve got no purpose,
no reason to wake up in the mornings,
I`ve got nothing.

No job, no friends, no love life, no one
to talk to, from career wise to love wise
my life is empty and that finally has
sunken in

My biggest fear is that I will never be able to hold your hand, to feel your skin close to mine, to have the possibility to give you everything I can, to see those faces light up when I enter the room, I fear I will never hear you laugh, I fear I will never be able to give you hope on a bad day, to hold you when the world is to much and no words are enough for the only thing that can help us is our arms around each others, I fear I will never be able to look into your eyes to wonder what your world looks like, I fear that you all will never be born for all I want is to hold you in my arms for all I am would be yours, I fear I will never be allowed to give you that

Can`t you see that i`m standing here
watching as my life is passing by when
all other lives live on without even
realizing who I am

My love only exists within me, for you to
find it is like solving a puzzle where too
many pieces are lost

To be known by no one is what my life
has always been, no one that has tried
to get inside of my shell I only remain a
mystery people never cared for

Never to have someone to guide me through hard times, never to have anyone who knows how my brain works, never to have anyone that could show me the different ways of life for all life the roads I have walked have been empty

You don't want to know the real me, I am dark, I am fearful, I am a cloud of destruction and I am not worth the effort it takes

Chapter Two
The war
The battle between my two sides

Nothing in this life matters if you are not
happy,
People, money, a career can be great
but nothing of that matters for you
should always come first

The world is hateful, it is grim and cruel
but if that is all you see then that is all
you have in your heart for the world can
be beautiful, loving and helpful but if
that is not what is within your heart then
you will never see it

Bring me light, bring me darkness, bring
me everything you`ve got. I have
survived this long fighting back
everything, nothing can stop me
anymore

Love will bring me to tears, it will make me see life in a way you can`t understand if you haven't felt love, that's the thing with love it will bring you all the joy in the world but it will never last

I need someone that can love me
unconditionally for who I am. I`ve seen
struggle, i`ve seen pain and darkness, I
know i`m not close to perfect. I struggle
against my own mind and I make
mistakes, all I know is I'm trying to
improve. I love myself but there is so
many things about me that I can't seem
to fix, all i`m is a massive scar that can
never seem to heal, I never seem to
experience real love

Cry if you want, Cry if you need , cry
without a reason, cry to grow. In order to
heal we need to suffer, to suffer we
need to shed our tears. Tears of joy,
tears of sadness, tears of darkness and
brightness

Listen when my heart speaks to you, listen to how it cries to you to know the pain we have felt wasn't for nothing. My heart cries though i`m not sad, my heart has not been broken. It cries for all of the pain we needed to go through that young. My heart cries knowing my younger self didn't suffer for nothing

Dry those tears on your cheek, grab
your heart up from the floor, it's time to
go to war

- A fight against yourself

I might be weak, hurt, broken and my
eyes sees blurry but the pain i`ve had it
can`t win over me so nothing can make
me stay down on the ground

The pain you've had if it's from your own
decisions or others have hurt you, you
can never let that define who you are.
The pain can be used to light the fire
but if you let it be the water it's because
you let it win

Victory is never something you can control. Sometimes a defeat will happen but winners rise when they lose and never ever give up on their dream

Love will hurt you, it will fail you and it will punish you but if you don't fight for your love your love will never stay, fight for your love or it will punish you over and over again

The story I will tell myself as I take my finale breaths will be. I didn't win but I never gave up

Save your pain for a while
I will carry it

Remember
I will love my life as long as I can and I
will hold on to it til the day I die.
Remember the sweet old days,
remember the glory days, remember
who we were and where we were. I will
remember you until my last breath is
gone, until my last step is taken. I will
remember you for as long as I can but I
know you won't remember me

No one sees the tears of a broken man, no one feels for he has lost it all, no one looks into their eyes and says it will all be okay, stand up and be a man that's all we've ever been

You are going to lose fights maybe you
will even lose all of them but the war
yeah you might lose that too but if you
stop fighting you will lose yourself

I wake up everyday with an empty heart. The heart that should carry me out of bed and push me towards new boundaries is too weak and the rest of my body has to carry it out in life

Can you take me back home so I can
feel my sorrow again, will you take me
back to you so I can feel the pain you
once caused, take me back so that I
can feel my frustration one more time,
i`m standing here in front of you so you
can scream it all to my face

Let there be hope in your heart, let there be no darkness in your mind and let there be dreams for tomorrow or it will die with you today

The day has come, the day my life will turn upside down, the day I will be chasing something greater than myself. My fear will no longer seem to exist in my life

What`s within my heart is love, what`s
within my heart is who I really am. No
matter how hard I try, no one can see
who i`m for they are only scraping the
surface and judging me long before i`m
known. No love enters my heart from
others but it still exists in me

Dying is not a choice you can make for it hunts us all down, not living is a choice that you make every single day

Not chasing your own happiness
everyday is a crime you will regret
everyday of your life

My life can't start, I wait and wait for the
day that never comes, there is a day far
ahead in the distance where I can finally
harvest these sweet, juicy apples and
feast on it`s meat

Can you see me standing here watching you, can you feel my presence within your skin, do you feel my cold breath in your neck, can you see my dark gloomy eyes staring at you, do you see me?
- The devils having a feast on my expense

Waking up and getting out of bed are sometimes the hardest task but it's a must

The life I live is lonely, the only time I
feel at home is when I touch myself for
without it what even am I, I am not living
for I only exist. There is only one thing I
want in my life to have a pair of arms
wrapped around me

I can't see what you see, you can`t see
what I see but our lives can be pretty
good even though our way of life is
different

We grow up with hope of excitement in our hearts, that the whole world is out there waiting for us and everything seems possible. The excitement dies only a few years later and our minds are hit with a swing of reality, suddenly that hope and excitement was gone, for most of us we never find it again

We stand up on our legs because our
arms are too weak to carry us, we walk
a thousand miles for that is what our
feets were meant to do, our souls are
not meant to carry the weight of lost for
that we have our heart, we are not
broken nor weak we have only been
using ourselves in the wrong way

My head is spinning, my legs are shaking, my body fails to respond and down on the ground I fall, tired, weak and almost gone I am, somehow I always manage to stand up again for it all starts over tomorrow

Fighting the world, fighting the battle in yourself, fighting back at every obstacle you encounter you face, it's never about surviving but fighting for the chance to live

You see me standing in the corner
looking into the wall, cramped in the
small corner. The security and the
safety of the corner keeps me safe from
the world but needing to turn around
and leave our safe space we need to
live

You fell in love with the idea of me, you
fell in love with a man you had hoped
was as good in life as in your dreams,
you fell in love with everything I said
and did but never who I was, the person
I was, who I am you never loved, for all I
did you only loved who you thought I
was but most important you never loved
my soul, my energy, you only loved my
words and that is never enough for love

Bring me tears of joy, sing my song til
the day I die, save your time and waste
no more on me, bring the world to an
end so we don't have to suffer anymore

Try and break me you do, stare into my soul and you will see what kind of monster you have come up against

I build the towers just for them to get torn down, I heal my broken leg just for it to break again, I look up to the sky and I wonder how this world could bring me all of this pain I have suffered from. We build, we fix and we heal time and time again every time we get better and stronger for it

Fearing death is natural for all of us do
so but fearing life is a hate crime
towards yourself

The world around us is broken for those
who can see it but for those who can`t
are already too broken by this world for
they can not see anything wrong with
this place

Amongst the people I live I find no hope, I only find sorrow for the broken souls, I only see the dark turns everyone is to scared to go, I only feel the pain the others leave behind for they didn't have time to deal with, the world is in ruins and all we can do is find our way through the broken houses onto a path that haven't been ruined for us to walk on

We do not belong in this world among
these people, we do not want what the
rest of the world wants, we do not give a
shit for all we are looking for is peace in
our souls, a burning fire in our hearts
and love through our bones for all we
know that lives on but all other things
dies when our body does but you live
on in those lost souls you ones were

Among these people we feel lost, among our equals our hearts wants what no one else want, our hearts know where we want to go and where we belong but we can't get there, we seek the seven seas to find the place where we finally can rest but that place for us we can never find in places, in others or in things, real souls that is fully connected with your heart can only find their home through the thousands of stories buried in your soul waiting to ones again be read and understood, the bodies and energies that carried this very soul can finally get their rest if you are brave enough to dig that far down

I wish I had your strength to carry me
today

Chapter Three
Love might exist
Finding the love in me

Love is simple, if you love me for who I am I will give you the entire world for the one who loves me I will give them my entire heart and soul for within me lies the whole world of love and nothing greater can be given

We all will die, as long as I make myself
proud I don't care how or when

Can love become anything else? The love that we carry for each other, for ourselves. The love we hold will always be there no matter what happens, the love will stand even when you are hurt and broken. The love will never be less but it can be so much more

Tell me how much you love me without your words, I want every bone within you screaming to me how much you love me. If I can feel your body aching of love towards me only then I know the love that you carry for me is all I have ever wanted and there is not a word in the world that could make me feel that way

The light that strikes your cheek on a
cold winter day is what love should be,
the warm feel of the sun even for only a
few minutes is enough to get you
through anything the world has to offer

That's the thing with love it almost kills you but if you can survive it nothing else then love will forever be in you, love will never last forever and therefore if you miss it it's gone forever, grab it while you can and love hard and passionate for the time you can

Love can be felt, it can be heard, it can be sensed. Love has the possibility to be experienced in so many ways

I want your face to light up when you
see me, I want to feel your arms
wrapped around me, I want to feel your
heart pressed to mine, I want to hear
your soul speak to mine

Let me take your hand and guide you towards my heart. Let me show you the key to my soul. I will show you what no one else knows, I will show you who I am because when I'm gone you will hold me in your arms. Let me show you my heart,
I will never give up for you, all I am will always be with you. Let there be light for you, let there be love for us

Love me if you can
I will try it myself

Our hearts can bend stars, it can heal
bodies, powerful enough to destroy the
world even though our love can never
be for you gave up too soon

Remember the good times you had with
yourself,
Now go and find some new ones to
remember

Remember the sacrifices you have made, remember everything you have been fighting for, remember all of the choices you have made for you believed in love over everything else, anything less is unworthy to exist in your heart

Don't ever let your pain feel anything
less than someone else`s. The pain you
had to endure is yours and it can only
be felt by you, no one but you

If you love me, love me with all of you, I
need to feel your entire body aching for
it needs me, that your mind speaks to
mine even when we are gone, if you
love me you need to love all of me, all of
my mistakes, all of my failures and
everything i`ve gone through, your love
for me it has to be all you have to give,
your love must be all committed to my
love

Can you love me for who I am?
If you can
show me the hearts of a thousand
souls

I will love you till my own days are
counted, I will love you for my heart has
ached a lifetime for a home, I will love
you for you is all I fight for

- My heart speaks to me

I will say it on a day when both of us
can hear it, for us that day is always

Love yourself first, for the first and last
one to love is none but you

The existence of man would seem to
die if it wasn't for love, for all love
makes us stand up for all we have ever
stood for

I watch you in my sleep, I see how your
body drifts away to the sound of the
music, nothing could be more perfect

- Dancing on my own

Hold my hand when I need you, wrap
your arms around me when I can`t
sleep, send me into your heart and let
me rest there,
I need that

Touch my hand to see my heart, look into my eyes to find my soul, feel my presence and I will always be with you. You don't need to remember my voice, my face or even my name, you don't need to remember what I have told you, you don't have to remember how my hand feels as it touches yours or how my arms feel round you, the only thing you have to remember is that you will forever have a piece of me in you. Say my name and I will always answer, if you need me i`m there, it's impossible to break our bond for we are not connected through blood but through our souls, blood dies but souls always live on

Come and sit down next to me for a
while, here you will always have a home
and a place where you belong

Nothing in this world matters if it doesn't contain love, for it is stronger than all of us, it breaks all the boundaries and will exist long after we are gone

I don't want to be seen nor heard or felt,
all I want is to leave a piece of my heart
in yours

Life is right in front of me and how I feel
to throw myself out and fly. I ask myself
if i`m ready for it, I don`t know but
without the jump of faith there is no life
for me

A better life
My heart is pounding, my mind is
aching, I know where I am but I don't
know where to go. Is there a better life I
ask myself but as my heart is filled with
joy I don`t care, for this life is more than
good for me. I can see the light but I
can't seem to reach it, that does not
bother me anymore. I am who I am and
I will never change that, all my doing in
this life has brought me to this place
and I don't regret the things I have done

The day that I die is the day when all of my memories will come back to me, all of the memories I have created with myself and with all of the people I love. What I have done in all of these memories has very little meaning for the only thing that does is that I'm proud of what I have done and all of the people I have been able to meet. I will die naked and poor just the way I was born into this world, we have nothing here to take only to learn as much as we can. I take my last breath I look around of what my life has been and I have to say it has been fucking good

The world that we see with our eyes is
not the world our souls can see. The
deepest and most beautiful things we
can imagine can be seen with our souls
for our eyes are only made for living.
Close your eyes and the whole world
will open up for you

Our struggles and our pain is ours, for
no one can tell us how we should feel

"Nothing matters without friends"
Everything matters all the time for you
have yourself always and that is always
more than enough

Give me that little light of hope I need
and everything I do from here will be for
you

We seek all of our lives far and wide for
a place where we belong out in the
world to find that it's empty and the
place we have been looking for all this
time exists wherever we can be
ourselves

Love is ingrained into who we are, it is part of our lives, just like we eat and sleep love is essential for us to live

Love for all you have, love for all you got, love for love is all we have, on our deathbed there will be thousands of things we would have wanted to do but none of them matter as love does. Regret not skydiving but you never want to regret not loving enough

My ears can hear what you say but they can not hear what you feel because that is only for the heart

All alone into the forest I go to find a
place where I belong, the place of
belonging is not within people or places
it's about finding it in you

In silence is where I grow, in silence is where I find my peace, in silence is where I rest, in silence is where I found where I belong, silence strengthens me, it keeps me fighting for yet another day, its within every bone in my body, its ingrained in my dna, silence is beautiful for nothing bad is born in silence other then our souls

Learning to love yourself is the greatest gift you can give to you, for that love is the only love that will last a lifetime

We love, we hope, we dream, these things are not necessary for survival but they are crucial for living any life

Feel how my heart pumps out all of that
love for you, feel how my heart is
hurting when you are gone, feel how my
heart has ached a lifetime for someone
to love, feel my heart and feel
everything I can give to you, my heart is
now your heart

Love yourself every fucking day for what
you know this could be your last day
and to not love yourself on your last day
is something you will never forgive
yourself for

I want you to die in my arms because
the pain of losing your soulmate is a
great deal. If I can take that pain away
from you and give it to myself I will do
so everyday for that is the type of lover I
am

Loving yourself will be one of the hardest tasks we all have to face, for many it never happens, we somehow can never get over our flaws and imperfections, life is never about perfection it's about being a person a human being that you can be proud of and someone you can lift up on a bad day, can you be your own best friend then all other problems will more or less fix themselves

Patience is key for great things take
time and our largest creation is
ourselves, that is something that we
always have to work on

I was weak, I was down, you brought
me down to this place but you were also
the one who got me back up when no
one else could

- Loneliness can kill your soul but if it
doesn't then all of life will lay ahead of
you

Great things always come to an end but
for life all ends means there will be a
new beginning when the sun rises again

I lift my head up towards the stars to see that nothing we do, nothing we create, nothing we ever will make with our lives matters, the stars existed long before us and will so long after we are gone for all we do, all we are will never matter but it all matters right now so love as much as you can, enjoy every hard time and every beautiful moment you see, life matter now but only for this very short time in the universe

We see our lives, we see our days, we
see what the world has to offer when we
open our eyes, we see the seasons
changing as life dies and always comes
back to life, we see our hope for the
future, we see a time when our lives will
be all that we have ever dreamt of, we
see life for all that it is, beautiful

All of our dreams are yet to be but
seeing what life has to offer right here
it's hard not to fall in love with it

When the time comes for us to finally
say goodbye all we have is the love for
ourselves no one else`s love exists in
our lives more than ours and at this very
last moment we get to share with
ourselves for a last time, love for the
time we had, love for the man we
became, love for all the times we loved
ourselves

Lifting our heads high up to the sky for
the proudness of who we have
managed to become, our work, our
dedication, our sacrifices, proud for all
we are

When I die, when I wake up I know i`m
going to die
All the work I do is towards my death
but before I get there I will feel more
alive then I have ever felt before

My knees falls down on the wet cold ground, my hands land down, my head drops and all my body collapses, the pain is gone, the dark clouds that filled the skies are gone and it's all blue and sunny, the time has come i'm finally out of the storm and all that is in front of me is warmness and hope

Some of us were made to be alone for
we have the strength to get through it all
even though many times we don`t think
we have the strength and many times
were we wish we had someone to talk
to and someone who understands us for
what we are but life for some will never
be that and for us we have to remind
ourselves of the strength that we carry
for we have got this far with it

Let love live
Long live love
Life long love lives

I leave you with the final words I`d give to myself, Love is hard to find, love is difficult to retain, love is hard to always give but love we need in order to live, to survive and to simply just exist this very day, let your love be shown, let your love be heard and let it be felt by yourself not some days but all the days we get to spend here

Chapter Four
The forest
The place where I belong

The power of nature

You give me the strength I need to move on, you give me the power to get that extra mile and you give me all I need to live. You will forever be a big part of my life and the biggest part of the person I am today. I take my dip in the November dark, the only things that lights up are the few houses I can see across the lake, everybody sitting at home without realizing what happens outside of their houses. In this very moment it's only me that exists, no one else, I feel the energy that nature gives me and it's the same as being reborn. No one lives in this world, only humans exist and with this act of nature I show how i`m not a part of that. I belong here in nature as we all do but for most are scared of finding themselves

Around the trees I'd be living, I breathe the forestry smell from the trees, I hear the birds in the background, I see the two squirrels chasing each other from branch to branch, here I belong, here I was made and nowhere else should I be. I was made to be wild here

The energy I have, the energy I give was made here and all I do, I do it for you, my life, my existence and I can breathe for you give me the oxygen, you are everything I am and I will forever be all of you

-The lungs of the forest.

Realizing I was not alone made me tear up, it made me see the world in a new way, it made me believe in something we can not see or hear but only feel in our hearts, to believe we have to or all our dreams will be gone, the world is wider then we have ever known

I hear their whispering in my heart, I understand the sorrows of those before me, I feel the gratitude of those energies I took time to understand

- The broken souls that were forgotten

On my way back home I can find myself again after I was sent away for two whole decades in a world I was never made for

I can breathe, I can dream, I can spend
another day here, I can realize the
nightmares are over for I have found
myself and I have found my life

No more fears
No more tears though I have a life to
live

Knowing my time is worth, knowing my place in this world is valid, Knowing I have a place I can call home, a place I can give everything of myself and get all of it and much more back

I sit down next to you to dry your tears
knowing the life we create is worth
every tear we shed, every pain in our
muscles and all the blood we lose

If I could turn the time back I would do it
all again,
the person I am,
the life I have would never exist without
it

In the past I woke up on days I didn't
want to wake up to do things I didn't
want to do, I now I wake up on days I
don't want to wake up so I can do things
I want to do

I want to die in your arms for I am
nothing without you and with you I want
to rest my final time

- Buried with the trees

Without you I can't see the world I want
to see, you give me the eyes I need, the
world your eyes see are bright of light
that goes beyond our human eyes

Take your time to watch me, to look into my eyes so you can see the world that I see

We live,
we breathe,
we die,
we soar and we surrender ourselves to
the unknown so we can live the known

Come sit down with me for a while so all
your worries can be gone for a minute
or two

My two hands were made to work with
you,
never against

There is no time to die anymore,
it's time to go out to get our work done
before winter is here

Our hearts have always been
intertwined with each other therefore I
have always had a helping hand

Alone in this world we all are but lonely
none of us ever is,
our soul finds a home wherever we are

No more will I give up on this world, no
more

- Life is difficult but so beautiful

Trapped in the dark even the slightest of
light changes the room completely,
the light gives us hope to know life
exists in the darkest of times

The strength I need to wake up
everyday is mare but with you next to
me I feel everything is possible

The dreams we have can keep us
captivating of our own possibilities until
we realize the dreams were simply just
dreams

Life is too beautiful to be this difficult but
nothing that is beautiful can be
appreciated unless there is a time of
difficulties leading up to it

Happiness hits me so I can enjoy it for
as long as I can

The joy that fills my heart is the first for me, the warm and safe feels I have are nothing but pure and I know it will not last forever, nothing of what the future holds bother me for all that matters is this moment where I am at home in myself

The horrors of yesterday will never be
forgotten but they will be overshadowed
by the lights of tomorrow

The more I walk through the forest the
more I find about who I am, the more I
find about how I want to live my life, the
more I find out what I am capable of
doing, I walk the same path but it's
never about the path it's about how you
can see the same path differently every
time for you dig deeper into yourself to
find who you are, the core of you will be
found in the simplest of times and
places

The path guides my feets but the forest
guides my heart to where I belong

The time here is soon over and all of
this will be over so it's time to find a new
adventure we can start chasing

I am sorry my friend but my life has to
come before you,
my life I must prioritize or I will not have
a life to live

Our work has been completed,
our time here is done but we will never
have to say goodbye to each other for
our hearts will always be together

To exist in this world we can simply just
live but to live we can't just exist

I am down on my feet again trying to
stay that way for life is so much more
enjoyable when you keep yourself
grounded to your love

My heart is empty with my old demons,
there is nothing for them to live off
anymore,
all that lived there had to die so my
heart could change to fit the new
creatures that wants to make it their
home

The snow covered paths in the forest
are slowly melting for the spring to
arrive.
I followed them home for the last time
before it`s time to leave the snowy time
for now and find the warm and soft path
that was made for us to walk with our
bare feets

The nightmare I entered in long before I
knew it has carved marks on all of my
body to see where I come from,
to know where I need to head in life,
the nightmare I never thought would
end has turned to a life,
a person I love and a story I can`t stop
writing

I have my hope, I have my love,
I have myself and as long as that exists
in my life so will I,
The world is filled with too much shit to
not see that all that matters is the
simplest of things right below your nose

The world can be seen in so many
ways, so close your eyes and find yours
for it will be the most honest way to see
life, that will always be the most
beautiful way

I don`t always love my life but I love myself, I don`t always love what I do but I love myself, I don't always love myself but I love myself, life is filled with misery but you will always love yourself

A letter to myself

I never gave up on myself, I will always love you for all your mistakes, for all your bad doings, for every time you let yourself down, I love you for all your imperfections, all you have ever done for everyone else and yourself, I love you for no one is you and no one will be, I love you for you never strive for perfection, you strive for love, joy and a life filled with it, I love you for you are my hero, I love you for you saved me and my future, I love you for you give me strength every single day, I love you for all the hard work you do, I love you for all the struggles you have had, I love you for the man you have become, I love you for staying on your feet even when you wanted to fall down, I love you for you always follow your heart over everything else, I love you for you are yourself, I love you so I hope you can remind yourself that once in a while

- Love is all we have for ourselves.

End Words

As I have sat down and written all of these poems over a few years of my life now I get thrown back to all of these different stories and some have been written with a smile on my face, some I have been full of ecstasy but most have been written with tears and pain in my heart. This is my heart so pure it can be, I have been broken and weak and some of these poems have been written in some of my most painful states and I can't say where I would be without them but I do know I would not be here where I am today without my poems. They have truly changed my life and so wherever you are in your life good or bad I couldn't recommend you more then to write yourself and don`t be like me ask for help when you're weak, ask for help when you need it, ask for help for then you know who really cares about you, ask for help for we can`t live life without others.

-Thanks/
Gabriel